The Neighborhood Book of Common Prayer

The Neighborhood Book of Common Prayer

For information, write to The Neighborhood Church, PO Box 5977,
Providence, RI, USA or info@thenbhd.org.

First printing 2021

The Neighborhood
P.O. Box 5977
Providence, RI 02903
www.thenbhd.org

Library of Congress Control Number: 2021907078

ISBN 978-1-6671-2757-6

9 781667 127576

Dedicated to the Neighborhood Church

May the God of peace himself sanctify you completely,
and may your whole spirit and soul and body
be kept blameless at the coming of our Lord Jesus Christ.
He who calls you is faithful;
he will surely do it.

Table of Contents

About This Book

This little book contains few of my own words but producing it has been a very personal journey. The book would stand alone just fine without this chapter, and maybe it would have been better with less of my direct input, but I felt that I should share some of my story in hopes that some experiences may encourage you in wherever your own journey has you right now.

How It All started

2018 was a rough year for me. I was a couple of years into our little church plant and was struggling with idealistic ambition meeting reality. Our family was going through some challenging times. And after years in management, I was in the process of moving into a "leader of leaders" position as a Director overseeing 4-6 managers and their respective teams.

The company I was with was in a rapid growth stage, acquiring multiple companies a year and building out a massive engineering department of over 300 globally, with a solid 40-50 directly under my supervision and many of the major processes for the other 250 being part of my upcoming charter. I was set to step into the new role in November of that year, and though it was a big undertaking, I was confident I would pull it off. For many years of my life, I lived by the motto "bite off more than you can chew, and then chew it." Stubbornly facing every challenge life threw at me with harder effort. And though I can confidently say at this point in my life I was not being swayed by materialism or greed, I was certainly flirting in my heart with the fleeting pleasures of success. The influence, power, and respect I had become things I was too ok with. My heart was starting to get far too much satisfaction to be healthy.

Though the warning signs seem clear as I look back (greatly increased insomnia, an expanding waistline, climbing heart rate and blood pressure, etc.), at the time I never expected to get sick. The week my promotion went into effect, my body finally gave in, and God showed me how easy it is for him to get the attention of even someone as stubborn as myself.

I don't remember what came first, the flu or the sinus infection or one of the ear infections or the bronchitis, but for the first time in my twelve-year career in Tech, I was bedridden for a week. After fighting it for too long, I finally listened to my wife and went to the doctors and was put on Prednisone, which greatly reduced the pain but came with its own set of problems that ended up weakening me for months. Walking up the staircase became a task I had to take multiple breaks to accomplish. For the first time in my life, there were multiple times in that valley that I honestly wasn't sure if I was going to die and I found myself anxiously and quietly making peace with God in between the intervals of fever and restless sleep.

Getting My Attention

That sickness consumed my Thanksgiving, and I was still recovering during Christmas. And for the first time in many years, my normal ambitious habit of performing an exhaustive personal yearly review and establishing goals and habits for the upcoming years was mostly tabled.

I don't think it had always been this way in every area of my life, but I had been doing everything in my flesh, in my own strength. My marriage, my parenting, attempting to lead a church, my career. My prayer life was quite literally non-existent outside of formalities. Everything I did needed a purpose, an agenda, needed some way for me to remain in control. And honestly, prayer didn't seem to "work".

But God had gotten my attention, that extended time of sickness had forced me to wrestle through some of what had been going on in my heart and relationship with him. So, my only major target for 2019 was to learn how to pray again. I changed my morning routine from a list of 5+ strategic habits to an untethered time of sitting in a specific chair in my bedroom and learned how to sit with my Father without an agenda. Slowly but surely, my prayer life was being developed. It started with simple unguided sitting and reflecting.

Entering a New Season

As the year continued, I read a couple of books on prayer, and tried different methods and rhythms. I grabbed "The Divine Hours" collection compiled by Phyllis Tickle as my first real exposure to fixed-hour guided prayer. I especially appreciated how it shaped the bedtime routine with the kids. I had previously not been exposed to the ancient practice of fixed-hour prayer (where specific periods throughout each day are assigned for prayer) and started to appreciate the practice. My wife gifted me with a little book by Dietrich Bonhoeffer entitled "Psalms: The Prayer Book of the Bible", where I was first introduced to the idea that the Psalms have been used for millennia by God's people across the languages and geographies, providing a kind of prayer vocabulary to so much of the shared human experience. Previously, the Psalms quite intimidated and even offended me. I preferred prose, where clear interpretations were possible and clear conclusions could be drawn. The Psalms are full of difficult statements, the extremes of human passions (even at times *undignified* passions). Many of them seemed to confront God in ways I didn't think were acceptable. Additionally, I had not spent much time praying "other people's prayers" in general and grew up with the assumption that each prayer must always be my own words for it to be prayer from me. What a thing to discover even Jesus often voiced his own prayers with the words of the Psalter. That springtime I was invited to spend some time at the Abbey of Genesee for silence and guided contemplation. My time at the monastery really opened up the ideas of fixed-hour prayer and the using the Psalms as prayer. I was able to join the monks for many of their fixed-hour prayer gatherings, where they have been simply and methodically chanting through all 150 Psalms each week together for decades. At the retreat house, I learned from some great local mentors, including Kevin Adams who authored "150 Finding Your Story in the Psalms" another great resource on the Psalms that I promptly gobbled up on my return from the retreat.

As Jesus began healing my own heart through extended time in prayer, I was growing in my ability to discern his guiding voice in my life more. After another time of retreat and prayer that summer, I knew my time at my previous job was in the concluding chapter. I quickly found another role that was a step down in salary and "prestige" but is a perfect fit for a bi-vocational church planter and father of 6, while still being very technically challenging and stimulating (and God has provided for our financial needs just fine regardless). My departure came as a shock to my boss who had been seeing my Director position as a steppingstone to Vice President within a year. If I hadn't been sure of the Father's leading, I don't think I would have said no to the opportunity to become a VP in a 1,400+ person company with hundreds of millions of yearly revenue, listed as one of the top 50 private SaaS companies in the nation. But I knew then and know now that was not God's path for my life. And the joy and freedom available when we are where we are supposed to be is worth far more than anything a job could offer.

And I was only able to start learning to understand and follow his subtle leadings at that level through spending significant amounts of time with him, allowing the beauty and mystery of the Psalms to wash over me and change my heart a hundred times over.

Consistently reflecting on the Psalms during the global and national chaos of 2020 taught me much about God's heart for justice and equality, about the dangers and transience of arrogant world leaders, about processing real fear and anxiety with him, about what waiting and hoping and agonizing for unanswered prayer looks like, about what worshipping the glorious one even directly in the storms of life looks like. It is no exaggeration to say that the Spirit has completely changed major aspects of me through the prayers he wrote in the Psalms.

The Project Begins

After coming back, I continued reading and praying the same Psalm list I learned at Genesee. My wife (who has always loved the Psalms), quickly grabbed hold of the opportunity to spend even more time in them. I wrote a Slack bot for our church plant that posts the relevant Psalms at specific times each day, and several others started dipping their toes and getting changed.

I appreciated how accessible The Divine Hours had been. Similarly, I had used the Common Prayer: A Liturgy for Ordinary Radicals by Claiborne and Wilson-Hartgrove, Celtic Daily Prayer by the Northumbria Community, and had been regularly using a similar format of liturgical prayer inspired from the Anglican tradition from The Order of Mission, of which my wife and I are permanent members. Each of these resources provided simple guided frameworks for praying, saturated in scripture. And each has blessed me in numerous ways. But I kept wondering how I could share the particular experience of the Psalms with others, without starting out with the seemingly insurmountable task of reading 150 Psalms a week.

Eventually, these two worlds came together, and the idea came to just take the same Psalm list we had joined the Abbey of Genesee in praying through and using it to form the content of a prayer book designed to be as accessible as the other resources mentioned had been.

When it came time to figure out the structure for an individual time of prayer - how it should open and close, what kinds of themes it should hit on, I came back to the instructions of Jesus on prayer when his disciples asked him how to pray. "Pray like this" he said and gave them the prayer commonly known as the Lord's Prayer or the Our Father. In it, Jesus was intending to simply give a single prayer to recite back to God repeatedly (though there is nothing wrong with that as one use), but he was giving us a *prayer framework*, a way of guiding our conversation with the Father.

If you have never seen the Lord's Prayer as a framework, it is generally understood as something like this:

Our Father who is in Heaven, hallowed be your name
Starting our Prayer with an acknowledgment of who God is: *Our Father* - the one who cares for us and provides for us. *who is in Heaven* - he is more glorious than we can comprehend, dwelling outside of our reality, full of power, full of wisdom. *Hallowed be your name* - a rightful acknowledgment that such a being deserves respect and honor and should be seen as different from the common things we typically discuss. We take time to praise this God. To simply tell him what he is like, thanking him for the beauty in creation, his works throughout the ages, his grace, his love.

Your Kingdom come, Your will be done, on earth as it is in Heaven
The Kingdom of God is the rule of God. It exists in the hearts of people who see him as creator and redeemer and submit to his upside-down way of living through humility and love. We take time to ask this broken world to more reflect the perfections of heaven - where his good and life-giving will is always followed. We look for where the "Kingdom of Men" has trampled the lowly, has abandoned the sick, has celebrated brutality and exploitation over love and servanthood, and we plead for his Kingdom to expand into those areas. We ask for the people we love who are still trapped in self-destructive mindsets and lifestyles to experience the freedom of living in his Kingdom under a different set of rules.

Give us this day our daily bread
A regular acknowledgment that he is the ultimate source of all of our provision. Our jobs, stuff, health, even the very breath in our lungs. After seeking his kingdom first, we then move into praying for the practicalities of life. We submit our human anxieties about that next promotion or that upcoming bill or that news from the doctor to a loving Father who cares and *is able to provide*. We ask for today, each new day. We don't take a stockpiling approach to life but embrace our dependence on his goodness.

And forgive us our debts, as we forgive our debtors
We recognize and confess the things in our own hearts that have contributed to the global problem of evil. The selfishness, the pride, the ways we have hurt others, the ways we failed to help others when we could. We name it, boldly and honestly, because we can only ever be free of what we can name. And we join our forgiving Father in being a conduit of his forgiveness to others around us. We refuse to let bitterness have the last word in our hearts, regardless of how people have hurt us. Sometimes we have to do this fresh every day for the same people, for years. But we do it, we keep bringing up their names and faces, and we keep verbalizing our intended forgiveness until it works its way through our soul and we are fully freed.

Lead us not into temptation, but deliver us from evil
We recognize that God orders our steps, and as we just finished reviewing our failures, we acknowledge the very strong potential that in our weakness we may repeat the same things again today or tomorrow. We ask for God's mercy to lead our day away from our weaknesses, protecting us from ourselves. We ask for listening ears to hear his voice and follow his way. We ask for strength to resist our own faulty impulses, or outside pressures to conform to the world as it is, or spiritual pressures to embrace twisted and false narratives of fear.

In this simple prayer that can be easily memorized by children, Jesus empowers in us a robust dialogue with the Father about the things closest to his heart and our own heart. Each day, this ancient form of prayer scrapes the new rust off my tired soul, reorients my heart away from the emptiness of materialism towards the vibrant worship of a living and mysterious God, and reminds me of my both significant and small place in the grand story he is weaving throughout the pages of human history. This prayer can never be exhausted and is too easily overlooked by a Church in search of innovation where repetition would be better suited.

And so the flow of each fixed-hour time of prayer in this book has taken the ancient shape of the Lord's prayer, filled with the even more ancient songs and poems of the Psalmists. Each day of the week, at 7 different specific markers in the day, we are invited to join in together in reading from the prayer book of the global and historic Church. And the flow of each page is designed to be able to serve the hurried few moments between errands, the quieter times where we can sit for 10 or 20 minutes, and even guide the extended opportunities of unhurried lingering that occasionally present themselves to us. And in each case, we can know we are joining a community of many others praying and reflecting on some of the same Psalms and themes at the same time.

My own prayer life is still far from perfect, and I certainly don't pull away for 30-45 minutes 7 times a day, 7 days a week. My time with God still has far too much restlessness, wandering thoughts and passions, plenty of doubts and fears, and more. But I will say that spending years letting the Psalms wash over my mind and heart have deeply changed me for the better. Even with the demands of Church planting, a large family, an involved day job, land-lording and extended family duties, I can honestly say that my pace feels slower and more intentional. I feel like more areas of my life are integrated into an ongoing conversation with Jesus. I feel like I know the Father's complex character more than ever. The change was large enough to motivate me to share it all with the wider Church and I hope my own story encourages you into exploring how your relationship with the Father can be deepened through rhythmic and sustained time with him in and through the Psalter.

Compiling this book was an absolute pleasure, as it was an excuse to spend even more time in the Psalms and really see firsthand how there is a Psalm for every prayer. I am grateful for the encouragement and editing assistance provided by my wife Karisa and my friend Sara Melucci. I am so thankful to the team at Resonate who provided such a life-shaping retreat to a weary Pastor at such a pivotal time. I am thankful to all of the authors listed and unlisted who encouraged my own journey of Faith and were a part of inspiring this work with their own insights.

I have chosen to utilize Tyndale's *New Living Translation* for all of the Psalm excerpts. As a father of 6, the readability and accessibility of the NLT is a huge asset in family worship. Additionally, as a community-focused Church plant, our Church is always seeking to cultivate an environment that is friendly to folks without much of a Church background themselves, and the NLT does a fantastic job of explaining terms that are unfamiliar to people from different backgrounds. There may come a day where we produce additional versions of this prayer book with one or two additional translations, as I am aware of how meaningful a favorite translation can be.

I pray that this little book can be used by our Father to bless and enrich your prayer life. I pray that your journey into the Psalms would be as shaping and healing and rejuvenating as it has been for me.

Joe Paravisini

How It Works

The Neighborhood's Book of Common Prayer is intended to be used by individuals, households, and communities for aiding the practice of fixed-hour prayer with the Psalms. At the core, this is a guide for praying with the Psalms. Though the Church has long seen the Psalms as her most precious book of prayer, regularly using the Psalms to shape our prayers has largely fallen out of practice with the average Christian. A fantastic introduction to the Psalms as the prayer of the Church can be found in Bonhoeffer's short work *Psalms: The Prayer Book of the Bible* nbhd.link/pttp

What is fixed-hour prayer?

Fixed-hour prayer is an ancient practice rooted in Judaism that adds rhythms of prayer at specific times each day. This is what the Psalmist refers to in Psalm 119:164 when he says that "Seven times a day do I praise you", and is what led Peter and John into the temple to prayer in Acts 3:1. While the content, frequency, and specific hours have fluctuated greatly over the millennia, and the practice itself is not specifically commanded in scripture, we believe there is wisdom and blessing to be found for modern folks who embark on including fixed-hour prayer in their spiritual rhythms. For a more in-depth history, Phyllis Tickle of the *Divine Hours* series has written a great resource available at nbhd.link/fixedhourprayer

How to use this book

This little prayer companion was designed to be simple yet flexible. It should be possible to pray through the basic prompts in a few minutes. In most of the offices, there are some promptings for engaging in unscripted prayer inspired by the verse, but there is still value in briefly praying God's own word back to him between tasks and responsibilities at home or work. Additionally, each office includes the same Psalm arrangement used by religious orders such as the Trappists throughout the ages which will take one through the entire Psalter each week. One really has three ways to use this book:

1. **Brief** (5 minutes) - Pray the verse excerpts in order
2. **Standard** (10-30 minutes) - Pray the verse excerpts, and spend several minutes on each section with prompts for specific prayer
3. **Extended** (30-60 minutes)- Slowly read and reflect on each of the Psalms, and then move into the Standard office flow

Additionally, in Appendix IV you will find a section for keeping track of ongoing specific requests aligned with the given sections of an office.

The Offices

The 7 times of daily prayer (or *Offices* from the Latin Officium, meaning *service* or *ceremony*) are listed below. Since Latin fluency has been waning for thousands of years, we opted to modernize the traditional names and add some additional context for each.

Midnight - Traditionally called *Vigils* (as in remaining "vigilant") or *Matins* (the early morning song of birds), the "night watch" is ideal for early risers, or anyone finding themselves awake when most others are asleep.

Wake Up - Traditionally called *Lauds* (praise), this is when the Church awakens herself with praises to the Father. The "First hour" of sunrise, traditionally observed at 6:00 am.

Start of Day - A brief office embarked right before starting the day's work. Traditionally called *Terce* (third hour of sunrise), this is typically observed around 9:00am.

Lunchtime - This office coincides with the noontime meal break. Traditionally called *Sext* (sixth hour of sunrise), this is usually observed around 12:00pm As this marks the halfway point of the day, this can also be a good time to practice the Examen (see Appendix III).

Afternoon Break Another brief office observed in late afternoon, perhaps over a coffee or tea break. Traditionally called *None* (ninth hour of sunrise), this office is usually observed around 3:00pm

Dinnertime - Typically before, during, or right after the evening meal. *Vespers* (or evening star) is celebrating the completion of the day's work and settling into the rest and reflection of the evening. Traditionally observed around 5:30pm or 6:00pm.

Bedtime - The bedtime office is the most flexible and consistent. It is flexible in that it has no set time other than right before one retires. It is consistent in that the Psalms are the same each night, contributing to a peaceful bedtime routine easily adopted for children. Traditionally called *Compline* (or complete). Compline ends with "The Great Silence", continuing until dawn.

When beginning to engage in the habit of fixed-hour prayer, it is recommended to pick one or two offices (often Lauds and Compline) to begin with, adding in the others as occasion allows. Adding in even a brief daily time of consistent prayer over coffee in the morning is still a wonderful step towards greater spiritual health and vitality, so start small enough where you feel sure you will continue on the busier days.

Conventions Used in daily offices

As much as possible the conventions in this book seek to match other traditional prayer books such as the Anglican *Book of Common Prayer*, *The Divine Hours* by Phyllis Tickle, and *Common Prayer: A Liturgy for Ordinary Radicals* by Claiborne and Wilson-Hartgrove.

Green - Section headings, not read out loud.

Bold - Bold text is read out loud (typically together if in a communal setting). It is either a reference to a prayer (such as Gloria Patri, or the Lord's Prayer), or the text itself to be spoken.

Standard - Words printed in standard font are intended to be read/prayed. If in a group, these are said out loud and speakers can alternate.

Italics - Notes in Italics denote verse references as well as additional directions. Initially, read the directions out loud in a group setting, but feel free to omit when everyone understands.

The Hours

Sunday - Midnight

Psalms: 95,1,2,3,119:1-8,16,18,119:9-16

Moment of Silence
I have calmed and quieted my soul *Ps. 131:2a*

Request for Presence
I cried out to the LORD,
   and he answered me from his holy mountain.
I lay down and slept,
   yet I woke up in safety,
   for the LORD was watching over me. *Ps. 3:4-5*

Doxology
Come, let us sing to the LORD!
   Let us shout joyfully to the Rock of our salvation.
Let us come to him with thanksgiving.
   Let us sing psalms of praise to him.
For the LORD is a great God,
   a great King above all gods. *Ps. 95:1-3*
Express thankful praise for who God is and what he has done

Gloria Patri

God's Kingdom
Only ask, and I will give you the nations as your inheritance,
   the whole earth as your possession.'" *Ps. 2:8*
Pray for God's kingdom to increase locally and globally

Provision
LORD, you alone are my inheritance, my cup of blessing.
   You guard all that is mine.
The land you have given me is a pleasant land.
   What a wonderful inheritance! *Ps. 16:5-6*
Bring practical needs and anxieties to the Father

Confession, Forgiveness & Reconciliation
Oh, that my actions would consistently
   reflect your decrees!
Then I will not be ashamed
   when I compare my life with your commands. *Ps. 119:5-6*
Repent to God for wrong done and good left undone

Holiness, Guidance & Protection
Oh, the joys of those who do not follow the advice of the wicked,
   or stand around with sinners,
   or join in with mockers.
But they delight in the law of the LORD,
   meditating on it day and night.
They are like trees planted along the riverbank,
   bearing fruit each season.
Their leaves never wither,
   and they prosper in all they do. *Ps. 1:1-3*
Request the Spirit's wisdom and strength to walk in God's ways

Closing Benediction
I called on the LORD, who is worthy of praise,
   and he saved me from my enemies. *Ps. 18:3*

Sunday - Wake Up
Psalms: 24,63,118,150,119:17-24

Moment of Silence
I have calmed and quieted my soul *Ps. 131:2a*

Request for Presence
In my distress I prayed to the Lord,
    and the LORD answered me and set me free. *Ps. 118:5*

Doxology
Praise the LORD!
Praise God in his sanctuary;
    praise him in his mighty heaven!
Praise him for his mighty works;
    praise his unequaled greatness! *Ps. 150:1-2*
Express thankful praise for who God is and what he has done

Gloria Patri

God's Kingdom
The earth is the LORD, and everything in it.
    The world and all its people belong to him. *Ps. 24:1*
Pray for God's kingdom to increase locally and globally

Provision
Because you are my helper,
    I sing for joy in the shadow of your wings.
I cling to you;
    your strong right hand holds me securely. *Ps. 63:7-8*
Bring practical needs and anxieties to the Father

Confession, Forgiveness & Reconciliation
Be good to your servant,
    that I may live and obey your word.
Open my eyes to see
    the wonderful truths in your instructions. *Ps. 119:17-18*
Repent to God for wrong done and good left undone

Holiness, Guidance & Protection
Who may climb the mountain of the LORD?
    Who may stand in his holy place?
Only those whose hands and hearts are pure,
    who do not worship idols
    and never tell lies.
They will receive the LORD's blessing
    and have a right relationship with God their savior. *Ps. 24:3-5*
Request the Spirit's wisdom and strength to walk in God's ways

Closing Benediction
Give thanks to the LORD, for he is good!
    His faithful love endures forever. *Ps. 118:29*

Covenant Prayer

Sunday - Start of Day
Psalms: 66,30

Moment of Silence
I have calmed and quieted my soul *Ps. 131:2a*

Request for Presence
Sing to the LORD, all you godly ones!
    Praise his holy name.
For his anger lasts only a moment,
    but his favor lasts a lifetime!
Weeping may last through the night,
    but joy comes with the morning. *Ps. 30:4-5*

Doxology
Shout joyful praises to God, all the earth!
    Sing about the glory of his name!
Tell the world how glorious he is. *Ps. 66:1-2*
Express thankful praise for who God is and what he has done

Gloria Patri

God's Kingdom
For by his great power he rules forever.
    He watches every movement of the nations;
    let no rebel rise in defiance. *Ps. 66:7*
Pray for God's kingdom to increase locally and globally

Provision
We went through fire and flood,
    but you brought us to a place of great abundance. *Ps. 66:12b*
Bring practical needs and anxieties to the Father

Confession, Forgiveness & Reconciliation
If I had not confessed the sin in my heart,
    the LORD would not have listened.
Praise God, who did not ignore my prayer
    or withdraw his unfailing love from me. *Ps. 66:18,20*
Repent to God for wrong done and good left undone

Holiness, Guidance & Protection
Let the whole world bless our God
    and loudly sing his praises.
Our lives are in his hands,
    and he keeps our feet from stumbling. *Ps. 66:8-9*
Request the Spirit's wisdom and strength to walk in God's ways

Closing Benediction
You have turned my mourning into joyful dancing.
    You have taken away my clothes of mourning and clothed me with joy,
that I might sing praises to you and not be silent.
    O LORD my God, I will give you thanks forever! *Ps. 30:11-12*

Sunday - Lunchtime
Psalms: 23,76,28

Moment of Silence
I have calmed and quieted my soul *Ps. 131:2a*

Request for Presence
I pray to you, O LORD, my rock.
　　Do not turn a deaf ear to me. *Ps. 28:1a*

Doxology
Praise the LORD!
　　For he has heard my cry for mercy.
The LORD is my strength and shield.
　　I trust him with all my heart.
He helps me, and my heart is filled with joy.
　　I burst out in songs of thanksgiving. *Ps. 28:6-7*
Express thankful praise for who God is and what he has done

Gloria Patri

God's Kingdom
You stand up to judge those who do evil, O God,
　　and to rescue the oppressed of the earth. *Ps. 76:9*
Pray for God's kingdom to increase locally and globally

Provision
The LORD is my shepherd;
　　I have all that I need. *Ps. 23:1*
Bring practical needs and anxieties to the Father

Confession, Forgiveness & Reconciliation
Listen to my prayer for mercy
　　as I cry out to you for help,
　　as I lift my hands toward your holy sanctuary. *Ps. 28:2*
Repent to God for wrong done and good left undone

Holiness, Guidance & Protection
Even when I walk
　　through the darkest valley,
I will not be afraid,
　　for you are close beside me.
Your rod and your staff
　　protect and comfort me. *Ps. 23:4*
Request the Spirit's wisdom and strength to walk in God's ways

Closing Benediction
Surely your goodness and unfailing love will pursue me
　　all the days of my life,
and I will live in the house of the LORD
　　forever. *Ps. 23:6*

Sunday - Afternoon Break

Psalms: 84,145

Moment of Silence
I have calmed and quieted my soul *Ps. 131:2a*

Request for Presence
O LORD God of Heaven's Armies, hear my prayer.
    Listen, O God of Jacob. *Ps. 84:8*

Doxology
I will exalt you, my God and King,
    and praise your name forever and ever.
I will praise you every day;
    yes, I will praise you forever.
Great is the LORD! He is most worthy of praise!
    No one can measure his greatness. *Ps. 145:1-3*
Express thankful praise for who God is and what he has done

Gloria Patri

God's Kingdom
Everyone will share the story of your wonderful goodness;
    they will sing with joy about your righteousness. *Ps. 145:7*
Pray for God's kingdom to increase locally and globally

Provision
When you open your hand,
    you satisfy the hunger and thirst of every living thing.
The LORD is righteous in everything he does;
    he is filled with kindness. *Ps. 145:16-17*
Bring practical needs and anxieties to the Father

Confession, Forgiveness & Reconciliation
The LORD is merciful and compassionate,
    slow to get angry and filled with unfailing love. *Ps. 145:8*
Repent to God for wrong done and good left undone

Holiness, Guidance & Protection
A single day in your courts
    is better than a thousand anywhere else!
I would rather be a gatekeeper in the house of my God
    than live the good life in the homes of the wicked. *Ps. 84:10*
Request the Spirit's wisdom and strength to walk in God's ways

Closing Benediction
For the LORD God is our sun and our shield.
    He gives us grace and glory.
The LORD will withhold no good thing
    from those who do what is right.
O LORD of Heaven's Armies,
    what joy for those who trust in you. *Ps. 84:11-12*

Sunday - Dinnertime

Psalms: 110,111,112,113

Moment of Silence
I have calmed and quieted my soul *Ps. 131:2a*

Request for Presence
Praise the LORD!
I will thank the LORD with all my heart
    as I meet with his godly people. *Ps. 111:1*

Doxology
Praise the LORD!
Yes, give praise, O servants of the LORD.
    Praise the name of the LORD! *Ps. 113:1*
Express thankful praise for who God is and what he has done

Gloria Patri

God's Kingdom
They share freely and give generously to those in need.
    Their good deeds will be remembered forever.
    They will have influence and honor. *Ps. 112:9*
Pray for God's kingdom to increase locally and globally

Provision
He gives food to those who fear him;
    he always remembers his covenant. *Ps. 111:5*
Bring practical needs and anxieties to the Father

Confession, Forgiveness & Reconciliation
He has paid a full ransom for his people.
    He has guaranteed his covenant with them forever. *Ps. 111:9a*
Repent to God for wrong done and good left undone

Holiness, Guidance & Protection
Praise the LORD!
How joyful are those who fear the LORD
    and delight in obeying his commands.
Their children will be successful everywhere;
    an entire generation of godly people will be blessed. *Ps. 112:1-2*
Request the Spirit's wisdom and strength to walk in God's ways

Closing Benediction
Who can be compared with the LORD our God,
    who is enthroned on high?
He stoops to look down
    on heaven and on earth.
He lifts the poor from the dust
    and the needy from the garbage dump.
He sets them among princes,
    even the princes of his own people!
He gives the childless woman a family,
    making her a happy mother.
Praise the LORD! *Ps. 113:5-9*

Monday - Midnight
Psalms: 96,37,73,119:25-32,40,50,71,119:33-40

Moment of Silence
I have calmed and quieted my soul *Ps. 131:2a*

Request for Presence
O LORD, I have come to you for protection;
     don't let me be disgraced. *Ps. 71:1*

Doxology
Publish his glorious deeds among the nations.
     Tell everyone about the amazing things he does.
Great is the LORD! He is most worthy of praise! *Ps. 96:3-4a*
Express thankful praise for who God is and what he has done

Gloria Patri

God's Kingdom
I have told all your people about your justice.
     I have not been afraid to speak out,
     as you, O LORD, well know.
I have not kept the good news of your justice hidden in my heart;
     I have talked about your faithfulness and saving power. *Ps. 40:9-10a*
Pray for God's kingdom to increase locally and globally

Provision
Commit everything you do to the LORD.
     Trust him, and he will help you. *Ps. 37:5*
Bring practical needs and anxieties to the Father

Confession, Forgiveness & Reconciliation
Keep me from lying to myself;
     give me the privilege of knowing your instructions. *Ps. 119:29*
Repent to God for wrong done and good left undone

Holiness, Guidance & Protection
Give me understanding and I will obey your instructions;
     I will put them into practice with all my heart.
Make me walk along the path of your commands,
     for that is where my happiness is found.
Turn my eyes from worthless things,
     and give me life through your word *Ps. 119:34-35,37*
Request the Spirit's wisdom and strength to walk in God's ways

Closing Benediction
But as for me, how good it is to be near God!
     I have made the Sovereign LORD my shelter,
     and I will tell everyone about the wonderful things you do.
Ps. 73:28

Monday - Wake Up

Psalms: 29,5,36,48

Moment of Silence
I have calmed and quieted my soul *Ps. 131:2a*

Request for Presence
O LORD, hear me as I pray;
    pay attention to my groaning.
Listen to my cry for help, my King and my God,
    for I pray to no one but you.
Listen to my voice in the morning, LORD.
    Each morning I bring my requests to you and wait expectantly.
Ps. 5:1-3

Doxology
Honor the LORD, you heavenly beings;
    honor the LORD for his glory and strength.
Honor the LORD for the glory of his name.
    Worship the LORD in the splendor of his Holiness. *Ps. 29:1-2*
Express thankful praise for who God is and what he has done

Gloria Patri

God's Kingdom
We had heard of the city's glory,
    but now we have seen it ourselves—
    the city of the LORD of Heaven's Armies.
It is the city of our God;
    he will make it safe forever. *Ps. 48:8*
Pray for God's kingdom to increase locally and globally

Provision
You care for people and animals alike, O LORD.
    How precious is your unfailing love, O God!
All humanity finds shelter
    in the shadow of your wings.
You feed them from the abundance of your own house,
    letting them drink from your river of delights. *Ps. 36:6b-8*
Bring practical needs and anxieties to the Father

Confession, Forgiveness & Reconciliation
Because of your unfailing love, I can enter your house;
    I will worship at your Temple with deepest awe. *Ps. 5:7*
Repent to God for wrong done and good left undone

Holiness, Guidance & Protection
Pour out your unfailing love on those who love you;
        give justice to those with honest hearts. *Ps. 36:10*
Request the Spirit's wisdom and strength to walk in God's ways

Closing Benediction
But let all who take refuge in you rejoice;
    let them sing joyful praises forever.
Spread your protection over them,
    that all who love your name may be filled with joy. *Ps. 5:11*

Covenant Prayer

Monday - Start of Day
Psalms: 9,10,15

Moment of Silence
I have calmed and quieted my soul *Ps. 131:2a*

Request for Presence
O LORD, why do you stand so far away?
   Why do you hide when I am in trouble? *Ps. 10:1*

Doxology
I will praise you, LORD, with all my heart;
   I will tell of all the marvelous things you have done. *Ps. 9:1*
Express thankful praise for who God is and what he has done

Gloria Patri

God's Kingdom
He will judge the world with justice
   and rule the nations with fairness.
Those who know your name trust in you,
   for you, O LORD, do not abandon those who search for you. *Ps. 9:8,10*
Pray for God's kingdom to increase locally and globally

Provision
The LORD is a shelter for the oppressed,
   a refuge in times of trouble. *Ps. 9:9*
Bring practical needs and anxieties to the Father

Confession, Forgiveness & Reconciliation
LORD, have mercy on me. *Ps. 9:13a*
Repent to God for wrong done and good left undone

Holiness, Guidance & Protection
Who may worship in your sanctuary, LORD?
   Who may enter your presence on your holy hill?
Those who lead blameless lives and do what is right,
   speaking the truth from sincere hearts. *Ps. 15:1-2*
Request the Spirit's wisdom and strength to walk in God's ways

Closing Benediction
LORD, you know the hopes of the helpless.
   Surely you will hear their cries and comfort them. *Ps. 10:17*

Monday - Lunchtime
Psalms: 120,121,122

Moment of Silence
I have calmed and quieted my soul *Ps. 131:2a*

Request for Presence
The LORD himself watches over you!
    The LORD stands beside you as your protective shade. *Ps. 121:5*

Doxology
I was glad when they said to me,
    "Let us go to the house of the LORD." *Ps. 122:1*
Express thankful praise for who God is and what he has done

Gloria Patri

God's Kingdom
For the sake of my family and friends, I will say,
    "May you have peace." *Ps. 122:8*
Pray for God's kingdom to increase locally and globally

Provision
My help comes from the LORD,
    who made heaven and earth! *Ps. 121:2*
Bring practical needs and anxieties to the Father

Confession, Forgiveness & Reconciliation
I took my troubles to the LORD;
    I cried out to him, and he answered my prayer. *Ps. 120:1*
Repent to God for wrong done and good left undone

Holiness, Guidance & Protection
He will not let you stumble;
    the one who watches over you will not slumber. *Ps. 121:3*
Request the Spirit's wisdom and strength to walk in God's ways

Closing Benediction
The LORD keeps you from all harm
    and watches over your life.
The LORD keeps watch over you as you come and go,
    both now and forever. *Ps. 121:7-8*

Monday - Afternoon Break
Psalms: 6,7,11

Moment of Silence
I have calmed and quieted my soul Ps. *131:2a*

Request for Presence
The LORD has heard my plea;
   the LORD will answer my prayer. Ps. *6:9*

Doxology
I will thank the LORD because he is just;
   I will sing praise to the name of the LORD Most High. Ps. *7:17*
Express thankful praise for who God is and what he has done

Gloria Patri

God's Kingdom
Gather the nations before you.
   Rule over them from on high. Ps. *7:7*
Pray for God's kingdom to increase locally and globally

Provision
Have compassion on me, LORD, for I am weak.
   Heal me, LORD, for my bones are in agony. Ps. *6:2*
Bring practical needs and anxieties to the Father

Confession, Forgiveness & Reconciliation
O LORD, don't rebuke me in your anger
   or discipline me in your rage. Ps. *6:1*
Repent to God for wrong done and good left undone

Holiness, Guidance & Protection
I come to you for protection, O LORD my God.
   Save me from my persecutors—rescue me! Ps. *7:1*
Request the Spirit's wisdom and strength to walk in God's ways

Closing Benediction
May all my enemies be disgraced and terrified.
   May they suddenly turn back in shame. Ps. *6:10*

Monday - Dinnertime

Moment of Silence
I have calmed and quieted my soul *Ps. 131:2a*

Request for Presence
I love the LORD because he hears my voice
   and my prayer for mercy.
Because he bends down to listen,
   I will pray as long as I have breath! *Ps. 116:1-2*

Doxology
Not to us, O LORD, not to us,
   but to your name goes all the glory
     for your unfailing love and faithfulness. *Ps. 115:1*
Express thankful praise for who God is and what he has done

Gloria Patri

God's Kingdom
Why let the nations say,
   "Where is their God?"
Our God is in the heavens,
   and he does as he wishes. *Ps. 115:2-3*
Pray for God's kingdom to increase locally and globally

Provision
What can I offer the LORD
   for all he has done for me?
I will lift up the cup of salvation
   and praise the LORD's name for saving me. *Ps. 116:12-13*
Bring practical needs and anxieties to the Father

Confession, Forgiveness & Reconciliation
Let my soul be at rest again,
   for the LORD has been good to me
He has saved me from death,
   my eyes from tears,
   my feet from stumbling. *Ps. 116:7-8*
Repent to God for wrong done and good left undone

Holiness, Guidance & Protection
I will keep on obeying your instructions
   forever and ever.
I will walk in freedom,
   for I have devoted myself to your commandments. *Ps. 119:44-45*
Request the Spirit's wisdom and strength to walk in God's ways

Closing Benediction
Praise the LORD, all you nations.
   Praise him, all you people of the earth.
For his unfailing love for us is powerful;
   the LORD's faithfulness endures forever.
Praise the LORD! *Ps. 117:1-2*

Tuesday - Midnight

Psalms: 97,49,82,119:49-56,42,43,68,119:57-64

Moment of Silence
I have calmed and quieted my soul Ps. 131:2a

Request for Presence
As the deer longs for streams of water,
   so I long for you, O God.
I thirst for God, the living God.
   When can I go and stand before him? Ps. 42:1-2

Doxology
May all who are godly rejoice in the LORD
   and praise his holy name! Ps. 97:12
Express thankful praise for who God is and what he has done

Gloria Patri

God's Kingdom
The LORD is king!
   Let the earth rejoice!
   Let the farthest coastlands be glad.
The heavens proclaim his righteousness;
   every nation sees his glory. Ps. 97:1,6
Pray for God's kingdom to increase locally and globally

Provision
Why should I fear when trouble comes,
   when enemies surround me?
They trust in their wealth
   and boast of great riches.
But as for me, God will redeem my life. Ps. 49:5-6,15a
Bring practical needs and anxieties to the Father

Confession, Forgiveness & Reconciliation
LORD, you are mine!
   I promise to obey your words!
With all my heart I want your blessings.
   Be merciful as you promised. Ps. 119:57-58
Repent to God for wrong done and good left undone

Holiness, Guidance & Protection
Your decrees have been the theme of my songs
   wherever I have lived.
I reflect at night on who you are, O LORD;
   therefore, I obey your instructions.
This is how I spend my life:
   obeying your commandments. Ps. 119:54-56
Request the Spirit's wisdom and strength to walk in God's ways

Closing Benediction
You who love the LORD, hate evil!
   He protects the lives of his godly people
   and rescues them from the power of the wicked.
Light shines on the godly,
   and joy on those whose hearts are right. Ps. 97:10-11

Tuesday - Wake Up

Psalms: 67,57,101,146

Moment of Silence
I have calmed and quieted my soul *Ps. 131:2a*

Request for Presence
Wake up, my heart!
   Wake up, O lyre and harp!
   I will wake the dawn with my song. *Ps. 57:8*

Doxology
Praise the LORD!
Let all that I am praise the LORD.
   I will praise the LORD as long as I live.
   I will sing praises to my God with my dying breath. *Ps. 146:1-2*
Express thankful praise for who God is and what he has done

Gloria Patri

God's Kingdom
He gives justice to the oppressed
   and food to the hungry.
The LORD frees the prisoners.
   The LORD opens the eyes of the blind.
The LORD lifts up those who are weighed down.
   The LORD loves the godly.
The LORD protects the foreigners among us.
   He cares for the orphans and widows,
   but he frustrates the plans of the wicked. *Ps. 146:7-9*
Pray for God's kingdom to increase locally and globally

Provision
But joyful are those who have the God of Israel as their helper,
   whose hope is in the LORD their God. *Ps. 146:5*
Bring practical needs and anxieties to the Father

Confession, Forgiveness & Reconciliation
Have mercy on me, O God, have mercy!
   I look to you for protection. *Ps. 57:1a*
Repent to God for wrong done and good left undone

Holiness, Guidance & Protection
I will lead a life of integrity
   in my own home.
I will refuse to look at
   anything vile and vulgar. *Ps. 101:2b-3a*
Request the Spirit's wisdom and strength to walk in God's ways

Closing Benediction
May God be merciful and bless us.
   May his face smile with favor on us. *Ps. 67:1*

Covenant Prayer

Tuesday - Start of Day
Psalms: 20,21,61

Moment of Silence
I have calmed and quieted my soul Ps. *131:2a*

Request for Presence
In times of trouble, may the LORD answer your cry.
 May the name of the God of Jacob keep you safe from all harm.
May he send you help from his sanctuary Ps. *20:1-2a*

Doxology
May we shout for joy when we hear of your victory
 and raise a victory banner in the name of our God. Ps. *20:5a*
Express thankful praise for who God is and what he has done

Gloria Patri

God's Kingdom
Some nations boast of their chariots and horses,
 but we boast in the name of the LORD our God.
Those nations will fall down and collapse,
 but we will rise up and stand firm. Ps. *20:7-8*
Pray for God's kingdom to increase locally and globally

Provision
How the king rejoices in your strength, O LORD!
 He shouts with joy because you give him victory.
For you have given him his heart's desire;
 you have withheld nothing he requested. Ps. *21:1-2*
Bring practical needs and anxieties to the Father

Confession, Forgiveness & Reconciliation
May your unfailing love and faithfulness watch over him.
 Then I will sing praises to your name forever
as I fulfill my vows each day. Ps. *61:7b-8*
Repent to God for wrong done and good left undone

Holiness, Guidance & Protection
O God, listen to my cry!
 Hear my prayer!
From the ends of the earth,
 I cry to you for help
 when my heart is overwhelmed.
Lead me to the towering rock of safety,
 for you are my safe refuge,
 a fortress where my enemies cannot reach me.
Let me live forever in your sanctuary,
 safe beneath the shelter of your wings! Ps. *61:1-4*
Request the Spirit's wisdom and strength to walk in God's ways

Closing Benediction
May he grant your heart's desires
 and make all your plans succeed…
May the LORD answer all your prayers. Ps. *20:4,5b*

Tuesday - Lunchtime
Psalms: 123,124,125

Moment of Silence
I have calmed and quieted my soul *Ps. 131:2a*

Request for Presence
I lift my eyes to you,
    O God, enthroned in heaven. *Ps. 123:1*

Doxology
What if the LORD had not been on our side? *Ps. 124:1a*
Express thankful praise for who God is and what he has done

Gloria Patri

God's Kingdom
Just as the mountains surround Jerusalem,
    so the LORD surrounds his people, both now and forever. *Ps. 125:2*
Pray for God's kingdom to increase locally and globally

Provision
Our help is from the LORD,
    who made heaven and earth. *Ps. 124:8*
Bring practical needs and anxieties to the Father

Confession, Forgiveness & Reconciliation
O LORD, do good to those who are good,
    whose hearts are in tune with you. *Ps. 125:4*
Repent to God for wrong done and good left undone

Holiness, Guidance & Protection
We keep looking to the LORD our God for his mercy,
    just as servants keep their eyes on their master,
    as a slave girl watches her mistress for the slightest signal.
Ps. 123:2
Request the Spirit's wisdom and strength to walk in God's ways

Closing Benediction
Those who trust in the LORD are as secure as Mount Zion;
    they will not be defeated but will endure forever. *Ps. 125:1*

Tuesday - Afternoon Break
Psalms: 12,26,86

Moment of Silence
I have calmed and quieted my soul Ps. 131:2a

Request for Presence
Bend down, O LORD, and hear my prayer;
    answer me, for I need your help. Ps. 86:1

Doxology
    I come to your altar, O LORD,
singing a song of thanksgiving
    and telling of all your wonders. Ps. 26:6b-7
Express thankful praise for who God is and what he has done

Gloria Patri

God's Kingdom
All the nations you made
    will come and bow before you, Lord;
    they will praise your holy name.
For you are great and perform wonderful deeds.
    You alone are God. Ps. 86:9-10
Pray for God's kingdom to increase locally and globally

Provision
Listen closely to my prayer, O LORD;
    hear my urgent cry.
I will call to you whenever I'm in trouble,
    and you will answer me. Ps. 86:6-7
Bring practical needs and anxieties to the Father

Confession, Forgiveness & Reconciliation
O Lord, you are so good, so ready to forgive,
    so full of unfailing love for all who ask for your help. Ps. 86:5
Repent to God for wrong done and good left undone

Holiness, Guidance & Protection
Teach me your ways, O LORD,
    that I may live according to your truth!
Grant me purity of heart,
    so that I may honor you. Ps. 86:11
Request the Spirit's wisdom and strength to walk in God's ways

Closing Benediction
The LORD's promises are pure,
    like silver refined in a furnace,
    purified seven times over. Ps. 12:6

Tuesday - Dinnertime
Psalms: 135,136,137,119:65-72

Moment of Silence
I have calmed and quieted my soul *Ps. 131:2a*

Request for Presence
Your name, O LORD, endures forever;
    your fame, O LORD, is known to every generation.
For the LORD will give justice to his people
    and have compassion on his servants. *Ps. 135:13-14*

Doxology
Praise the LORD, for the LORD is good;
    celebrate his lovely name with music. *Ps. 135:3*
Express thankful praise for who God is and what he has done

Gloria Patri

God's Kingdom
The LORD does whatever pleases him
    throughout all heaven and earth,
    and on the seas and in their depths.
He causes the clouds to rise over the whole earth.
    He sends the lightning with the rain
    and releases the wind from his storehouses. *Ps. 135:6-7*
Pray for God's kingdom to increase locally and globally

Provision
He remembered us in our weakness.
    His faithful love endures forever.
He saved us from our enemies.
    His faithful love endures forever.
He gives food to every living thing.
    His faithful love endures forever. *Ps. 136:23-25*
Bring practical needs and anxieties to the Father

Confession, Forgiveness & Reconciliation
I used to wander off until you disciplined me;
    but now I closely follow your word.
My suffering was good for me,
    for it taught me to pay attention to your decrees. *Ps. 119:67,71*
Repent to God for wrong done and good left undone

Holiness, Guidance & Protection
Beside the rivers of Babylon, we sat and wept
    as we thought of Jerusalem.
But how can we sing the songs of the LORD
    while in a pagan land? *Ps. 137:1,4*
Request the Spirit's wisdom and strength to walk in God's ways

Closing Benediction
Give thanks to the God of heaven.
    His faithful love endures forever. *Ps. 136:26*

Wednesday - Midnight
Psalms: 98,78,119:73-80,77,39,94,119:81-88

Moment of Silence
I have calmed and quieted my soul *Ps. 131:2a*

Request for Presence
I cry out to God; yes, I shout.
   Oh, that God would listen to me! *Ps. 77:1*

Doxology
Shout to the LORD, all the earth;
   break out in praise and sing for joy!
Sing your praise to the LORD with the harp,
   with the harp and melodious song,
with trumpets and the sound of the ram's horn.
   Make a joyful symphony before the LORD, the King! *Ps. 98:4-6*
Express thankful praise for who God is and what he has done

Gloria Patri

God's Kingdom
You are the God of great wonders!
   You demonstrate your awesome power among the nations. *Ps. 77:14*
Pray for God's kingdom to increase locally and globally

Provision
We are merely moving shadows,
   and all our busy rushing ends in nothing.
We heap up wealth,
   not knowing who will spend it.
And so, Lord, where do I put my hope?
   My only hope is in you. *Ps. 39:6-7*
Bring practical needs and anxieties to the Father

Confession, Forgiveness & Reconciliation
I know, O LORD, that your regulations are fair;
   you disciplined me because I needed it.
Now let your unfailing love comfort me,
   just as you promised me, your servant. *Ps. 119:75-76*
Repent to God for wrong done and good left undone

Holiness, Guidance & Protection
So each generation should set its hope anew on God,
   not forgetting his glorious miracles
   and obeying his commands. *Ps. 78:7*
Request the Spirit's wisdom and strength to walk in God's ways

Closing Benediction
O God, your ways are holy.
   Is there any god as mighty as you? *Ps. 77:13*

Wednesday - Wake Up
Psalms: 46,64,65,147

Moment of Silence
I have calmed and quieted my soul *Ps. 131:2a*

Request for Presence
The LORD of Heaven's Armies is here among us;
    the God of Israel is our fortress. *Ps. 46:7*

Doxology
What mighty praise, O God,
    belongs to you in Zion. *Ps. 65:1a*
Express thankful praise for who God is and what he has done

Gloria Patri

God's Kingdom
You faithfully answer our prayers with awesome deeds,
    O God our savior.
You are the hope of everyone on earth,
    even those who sail on distant seas. *Ps. 65:5*
Pray for God's kingdom to increase locally and globally

Provision
For he has strengthened the bars of your gates
    and blessed your children within your walls.
He sends peace across your nation
    and satisfies your hunger with the finest wheat. *Ps. 147:13-14*
Bring practical needs and anxieties to the Father

Confession, Forgiveness & Reconciliation
Though we are overwhelmed by our sins,
    you forgive them all. *Ps. 65:3*
Repent to God for wrong done and good left undone

Holiness, Guidance & Protection
What joy for those you choose to bring near,
    those who live in your holy courts.
What festivities await us
    inside your holy Temple. *Ps. 65:4*
Request the Spirit's wisdom and strength to walk in God's ways

Closing Benediction
The godly will rejoice in the LORD
    and find shelter in him.
And those who do what is right
    will praise him. *Ps. 64:10*

Covenant Prayer

Wednesday - Start of Day
Psalms: 14,17,52

Moment of Silence
I have calmed and quieted my soul *Ps. 131:2a*

Request for Presence
I am praying to you because I know you will answer, O God.
   Bend down and listen as I pray. *Ps. 17:6*

Doxology
I will praise you forever, O God,
   for what you have done.
I will trust in your good name
   in the presence of your faithful people. *Ps. 52:9*
Express thankful praise for who God is and what he has done

Gloria Patri

God's Kingdom
By the power of your hand, O LORD,
   destroy those who look to this world for their reward.
But satisfy the hunger of your treasured ones.
   May their children have plenty,
   leaving an inheritance for their descendants. *Ps. 17:14*
Pray for God's kingdom to increase locally and globally

Provision
But I am like an olive tree, thriving in the house of God.
   I will always trust in God's unfailing love. *Ps. 52:8*
Bring practical needs and anxieties to the Father

Confession, Forgiveness & Reconciliation
You have tested my thoughts and examined my heart in the night.
   You have scrutinized me and found nothing wrong.
   I am determined not to sin in what I say. *Ps. 17:3*
Repent to God for wrong done and good left undone

Holiness, Guidance & Protection
Show me your unfailing love in wonderful ways.
   By your mighty power you rescue
   those who seek refuge from their enemies.
Guard me as you would guard your own eyes.
   Hide me in the shadow of your wings. *Ps. 17:7-8*
Request the Spirit's wisdom and strength to walk in God's ways

Closing Benediction
Because I am righteous, I will see you.
   When I awake, I will see you face to face and be satisfied. *Ps. 17:15*

Wednesday - Lunchtime
Psalms: 126,127,128

Moment of Silence
I have calmed and quieted my soul *Ps. 131:2a*

Request for Presence
Those who plant in tears
   will harvest with shouts of joy.
They weep as they go to plant their seed,
   but they sing as they return with the harvest. *Ps. 126:5-6*

Doxology
Yes, the LORD has done amazing things for us!
   What joy! *Ps. 126:3*
Express thankful praise for who God is and what he has done

Gloria Patri

God's Kingdom
When the LORD brought back his exiles to Jerusalem,
   it was like a dream!
We were filled with laughter,
   and we sang for joy.
And the other nations said,
   "What amazing things the LORD has done for them." *Ps. 126:1-2*
Pray for God's kingdom to increase locally and globally

Provision
It is useless for you to work so hard
   from early morning until late at night,
anxiously working for food to eat;
   for God gives rest to his loved ones. *Ps. 127:2*
Bring practical needs and anxieties to the Father

Confession, Forgiveness & Reconciliation
How joyful are those who fear the LORD—
   all who follow his ways! *Ps. 128:1*
Repent to God for wrong done and good left undone

Holiness, Guidance & Protection
Unless the LORD builds a house,
   the work of the builders is wasted.
Unless the LORD protects a city,
   guarding it with sentries will do no good. *Ps. 127:1*
Request the Spirit's wisdom and strength to walk in God's ways

Closing Benediction
May the LORD continually bless you from Zion.
   May you see Jerusalem prosper as long as you live.
May you live to enjoy your grandchildren.
   May Israel have peace! *Ps. 128:5-6*

Wednesday - Afternoon Break

Psalms: 56,70,75

Moment of Silence
I have calmed and quieted my soul *Ps. 131:2a*

Request for Presence
But may all who search for you
    be filled with joy and gladness in you. *Ps. 70:4a*

Doxology
I praise God for what he has promised.
    I trust in God, so why should I be afraid?
    What can mere mortals do to me? *Ps. 56:4*
Express thankful praise for who God is and what he has done

Gloria Patri

God's Kingdom
We thank you, O God!
    We give thanks because you are near.
    People everywhere tell of your wonderful deeds. *Ps. 75:1*
Pray for God's kingdom to increase locally and globally

Provision
You keep track of all my sorrows.
    You have collected all my tears in your bottle.
    You have recorded each one in your book. *Ps. 56:8*
Bring practical needs and anxieties to the Father

Confession, Forgiveness & Reconciliation
For you have rescued me from death;
    you have kept my feet from slipping.
So now I can walk in your presence, O God,
    in your life-giving light. *Ps. 56:13*
Repent to God for wrong done and good left undone

Holiness, Guidance & Protection
May those who love your salvation
    repeatedly shout, "God is great!"
But as for me, I am poor and needy;
    please hurry to my aid, O God.
You are my helper and my savior;
    O LORD, do not delay. *Ps. 70:4b-5*
Request the Spirit's wisdom and strength to walk in God's ways

Closing Benediction
My enemies will retreat when I call to you for help.
    This I know: God is on my side!
I praise God for what he has promised;
    yes, I praise the LORD for what he has promised. *Ps. 56:9-10*

Wednesday - Dinnertime
Psalms: 138,139,140,119:89-96

Moment of Silence
I have calmed and quieted my soul *Ps. 131:2a*

Request for Presence
As soon as I pray, you answer me;
    you encourage me by giving me strength. *Ps. 138:3*

Doxology
I give you thanks, O LORD, with all my heart;
    I will sing your praises before the gods. *Ps. 138:1*
Express thankful praise for who God is and what he has done

Gloria Patri

God's Kingdom
Every king in all the earth will thank you, LORD,
    for all of them will hear your words.
Yes, they will sing about the LORD's ways,
    for the glory of the LORD is very great. *Ps. 138:4-5*
Pray for God's kingdom to increase locally and globally

Provision
The LORD will work out his plans for my life—
    for your faithful love, O LORD, endures forever.
    Don't abandon me, for you made me. *Ps. 138:8*
Bring practical needs and anxieties to the Father

Confession, Forgiveness & Reconciliation
Search me, O God, and know my heart;
    test me and know my anxious thoughts.
Point out anything in me that offends you,
    and lead me along the path of everlasting life. *Ps. 139:23-24*
Repent to God for wrong done and good left undone

Holiness, Guidance & Protection
Your eternal word, O LORD,
    stands firm in heaven.
Your faithfulness extends to every generation,
    as enduring as the earth you created.
Your regulations remain true to this day,
    for everything serves your plans. *Ps. 119:89-91*
Request the Spirit's wisdom and strength to walk in God's ways

Closing Benediction
I can never escape from your Spirit!
    I can never get away from your presence!
If I go up to heaven, you are there;
    If I go down to the grave, you are there.
If I ride the wings of the morning,
    if I dwell by the farthest oceans,
even there your hand will guide me,
    and your strength will support me. *Ps. 139:7-10*

Thursday - Midnight

Psalms: 99,38,25,31,119:97-104,103,106,119:105-112

Moment of Silence
I have calmed and quieted my soul *Ps. 131:2a*

Request for Presence
Your word is a lamp to guide my feet
  and a light for my path. *Ps. 119:105*

Doxology
Let all that I am praise the LORD;
 with my whole heart, I will praise his holy name.
Let all that I am praise the LORD;
 may I never forget the good things he does for me. *Ps. 103:1-2*
Express thankful praise for who God is and what he has done

Gloria Patri

God's Kingdom
Save us, O LORD our God!
 Gather us back from among the nations,
so we can thank your holy name
 and rejoice and praise you. *Ps. 106:47*
Pray for God's kingdom to increase locally and globally

Provision
Come quickly to help me,
 O Lord my savior. *Ps. 38:22*
Bring practical needs and anxieties to the Father

Confession, Forgiveness & Reconciliation
I am on the verge of collapse,
 facing constant pain.
But I confess my sins;
 I am deeply sorry for what I have done. *Ps. 38:17-18*
Repent to God for wrong done and good left undone

Holiness, Guidance & Protection
Show me the right path, O LORD;
 point out the road for me to follow.
Lead me by your truth and teach me,
 for you are the God who saves me.
 All day long I put my hope in you. *Ps. 25:4-5*
Request the Spirit's wisdom and strength to walk in God's ways

Closing Benediction
How great is the goodness you have stored up
 for those who fear you.
You lavish it on those who come to you for protection,
 blessing them before the watching world. *Ps. 31:19*

Thursday - Wake Up
Psalms: 81,80,108,147:12-20

Moment of Silence
I have calmed and quieted my soul *Ps. 131:2a*

Request for Presence
Turn us again to yourself, O God of Heaven's Armies.
    Make your face shine down upon us.
    Only then will we be saved. *Ps. 80:7*

Doxology
I will thank you, LORD, among all the people.
    I will sing your praises among the nations.
For your unfailing love is higher than the heavens.
    Your faithfulness reaches to the clouds.
Be exalted, O God, above the highest heavens.
    May your glory shine over all the earth. *Ps. 108:3-5*
Express thankful praise for who God is and what he has done

Gloria Patri

God's Kingdom
Glorify the LORD, O Jerusalem!
    Praise your God, O Zion!
For he has strengthened the bars of your gates
    and blessed your children within your walls.
He sends peace across your nation
    and satisfies your hunger with the finest wheat. *Ps. 147:12-15a*
Pray for God's kingdom to increase locally and globally

Provision
For it was I, the LORD your God,
    who rescued you from the land of Egypt.
    Open your mouth wide, and I will fill it with good things. *Ps. 81:10*
Bring practical needs and anxieties to the Father

Confession, Forgiveness & Reconciliation
Turn us again to yourself, O God of Heaven's Armies.
    Make your face shine down upon us.
    Only then will we be saved. *Ps. 80:3*
Repent to God for wrong done and good left undone

Holiness, Guidance & Protection
Oh, that my people would listen to me!
    Oh, that Israel would follow me, walking in my paths!
How quickly I would then subdue their enemies!
    How soon my hands would be upon their foes! *Ps. 81:13-14*
Request the Spirit's wisdom and strength to walk in God's ways

Closing Benediction
With God's help we will do mighty things
    for he will trample down our foes. *Ps. 108:13*

Covenant Prayer

Thursday - Start of Day
Psalms: 32,53,79

Moment of Silence
I have calmed and quieted my soul *Ps. 131:2a*

Request for Presence
Help us, O God of our salvation!
   Help us for the glory of your name.
Save us and forgive our sins
   for the honor of your name. *Ps. 79:9*

Doxology
We your people, the sheep of your pasture,
   will thank you forever and ever,
      praising your greatness from generation to generation. *Ps. 79:13*
Express thankful praise for who God is and what he has done

Gloria Patri

God's Kingdom
Who will come from Mount Zion to rescue Israel?
   When God restores his people,
   Jacob will shout with joy, and Israel will rejoice. *Ps. 53:6*
Pray for God's kingdom to increase locally and globally

Provision
   Let your compassion quickly meet our needs,
      for we are on the brink of despair. *Ps. 79:8b*
Bring practical needs and anxieties to the Father

Confession, Forgiveness & Reconciliation
When I refused to confess my sin,
   my body wasted away,
   and I groaned all day long.
Day and night your hand of discipline was heavy on me.
   My strength evaporated like water in the summer heat.
Finally, I confessed all my sins to you
   and stopped trying to hide my guilt.
I said to myself, "I will confess my rebellion to the LORD."
   And you forgave me! All my guilt is gone. *Ps. 32:3-5*
Repent to God for wrong done and good left undone

Holiness, Guidance & Protection
The LORD says, "I will guide you along the best pathway for your life.
   I will advise you and watch over you. *Ps. 32:8*
Request the Spirit's wisdom and strength to walk in God's ways

Closing Benediction
Rejoice in the LORD and be glad, all you who obey him!
   Shout for joy, all you whose hearts are pure! *Ps. 32:11*

Thursday - Lunchtime
Psalms: 129,130,131

Moment of Silence
I have calmed and quieted my soul *Ps. 131:2a*

Request for Presence
From the depths of despair, O LORD,
    I call for your help.
Hear my cry, O Lord.
    Pay attention to my prayer. *Ps. 130:1-2*

Doxology
I long for the Lord
    more than sentries long for the dawn,
    yes, more than sentries long for the dawn. *Ps. 130:6*
Express thankful praise for who God is and what he has done

Gloria Patri

God's Kingdom
But the LORD is good;
    he has cut me free from the ropes of the ungodly. *Ps. 129:4*
Pray for God's kingdom to increase locally and globally

Provision
I am counting on the LORD;
    yes, I am counting on him.
    I have put my hope in his word. *Ps. 130:5*
Bring practical needs and anxieties to the Father

Confession, Forgiveness & Reconciliation
LORD, if you kept a record of our sins,
    who, O Lord, could ever survive?
But you offer forgiveness,
    that we might learn to fear you. *Ps. 130:3-4*
Repent to God for wrong done and good left undone

Holiness, Guidance & Protection
LORD, my heart is not proud;
    my eyes are not haughty.
I don't concern myself with matters too great
    or too awesome for me to grasp. *Ps. 131:1*
Request the Spirit's wisdom and strength to walk in God's ways

Closing Benediction
O Israel, put your hope in the LORD—
    now and always. *Ps. 131:3*

Thursday - Afternoon Break

Psalms: 44,41

Moment of Silence
I have calmed and quieted my soul *Ps. 131:2a*

Request for Presence
Wake up, O Lord! Why do you sleep?
   Get up! Do not reject us forever. *Ps. 44:23*

Doxology
O God, we give glory to you all day long
   and constantly praise your name. *Ps. 44:8*
Express thankful praise for who God is and what he has done

Gloria Patri

God's Kingdom
O God, we have heard it with our own ears—
   our ancestors have told us
of all you did in their day,
   in days long ago *Ps. 44:1*
Pray for God's kingdom to increase locally and globally

Provision
Oh, the joys of those who are kind to the poor!
   The LORD rescues them when they are in trouble.
The LORD protects them
   and keeps them alive.
He gives them prosperity in the land
   and rescues them from their enemies.
The LORD nurses them when they are sick
   and restores them to health. *Ps. 41:1-3*
Bring practical needs and anxieties to the Father

Confession, Forgiveness & Reconciliation
"O LORD," I prayed, "have mercy on me.
   Heal me, for I have sinned against you." *Ps. 41:4*
Repent to God for wrong done and good left undone

Holiness, Guidance & Protection
Our hearts have not deserted you.
   We have not strayed from your path. *Ps. 44:18*
Request the Spirit's wisdom and strength to walk in God's ways

Closing Benediction
Praise the LORD, the God of Israel,
   who lives from everlasting to everlasting.
Amen and amen! *Ps. 41:13*

Thursday - Dinnertime

Psalms: 141,142,144,119:121-128

Moment of Silence
I have calmed and quieted my soul *Ps. 131:2a*

Request for Presence
O LORD, I am calling to you. Please hurry!
   Listen when I cry to you for help! *Ps. 141:1*

Doxology
Praise the LORD, who is my rock.
   He trains my hands for war
   and gives my fingers skill for battle. *Ps. 144:1*
Express thankful praise for who God is and what he has done

Gloria Patri

God's Kingdom
My eyes strain to see your rescue,
   to see the truth of your promise fulfilled. *Ps. 119:123*
Pray for God's kingdom to increase locally and globally

Provision
I cry out to the LORD;
   I plead for the LORD's mercy.
I pour out my complaints before him
   and tell him all my troubles.
When I am overwhelmed,
   you alone know the way I should turn. *Ps. 142:1-3a*
Bring practical needs and anxieties to the Father

Confession, Forgiveness & Reconciliation
O LORD, what are human beings that you should notice them,
   mere mortals that you should think about them? *Ps. 144:3*
Repent to God for wrong done and good left undone

Holiness, Guidance & Protection
Take control of what I say, O LORD,
   and guard my lips.
Don't let me drift toward evil
   or take part in acts of wickedness.
Don't let me share in the delicacies
   of those who do wrong. *Ps. 141:3-4*
Request the Spirit's wisdom and strength to walk in God's ways

Closing Benediction
May our sons flourish in their youth
   like well-nurtured plants.
May our daughters be like graceful pillars,
   carved to beautify a palace.
May our barns be filled
   with crops of every kind.
May the flocks in our fields multiply by the thousands,
   even tens of thousands,
   and may our oxen be loaded down with produce. *Ps. 144:12-14a*

Friday - Midnight
Psalms: 93,88,35,59,119:129-136,89,119:137-144

Moment of Silence
I have calmed and quieted my soul *Ps. 131:2a*

Request for Presence
O LORD, God of my salvation,
   I cry out to you by day.
   I come to you at night. *Ps. 88:1*

Doxology
But as for me, I will sing about your power.
   Each morning I will sing with joy about your unfailing love.
For you have been my refuge,
   a place of safety when I am in distress. *Ps. 59:16*
Express thankful praise for who God is and what he has done

Gloria Patri

God's Kingdom
Happy are those who hear the joyful call to worship,
   for they will walk in the light of your presence, LORD. *Ps. 89:15*
Pray for God's kingdom to increase locally and globally

Provision
With every bone in my body I will praise him:
   "LORD, who can compare with you?
Who else rescues the helpless from the strong?
   Who else protects the helpless and poor from those who rob them?" *Ps. 35:10*
Bring practical needs and anxieties to the Father

Confession, Forgiveness & Reconciliation
   My eyes are blinded by my tears.
Each day I beg for your help, O LORD;
   I lift my hands to you for mercy. *Ps. 88:9*
Repent to God for wrong done and good left undone

Holiness, Guidance & Protection
The teaching of your word gives light,
   so even the simple can understand.
Guide my steps by your word,
   so I will not be overcome by evil. *Ps. 119:130,133*
Request the Spirit's wisdom and strength to walk in God's ways

Closing Benediction
O my Strength, to you I sing praises,
   for you, O God, are my refuge,
   the God who shows me unfailing love. *Ps. 59:17*

Friday - Wake Up

Psalms: 100,51,143,148

Moment of Silence
I have calmed and quieted my soul *Ps. 131:2a*

Request for Presence
Hear my prayer, O LORD;
    listen to my plea!
    Answer me because you are faithful and righteous. *Ps. 143:1*

Doxology
Acknowledge that the LORD is God!
    He made us, and we are his.
    We are his people, the sheep of his pasture.
Enter his gates with thanksgiving;
    go into his courts with praise.
    Give thanks to him and praise his name. *Ps. 100:3-4*
Express thankful praise for who God is and what he has done |

Gloria Patri

God's Kingdom
Let every created thing give praise to the LORD,
    for he issued his command, and they came into being. *Ps. 148:5*
Pray for God's kingdom to increase locally and globally

Provision
For the glory of your name, O LORD, preserve my life.
    Because of your faithfulness, bring me out of this distress. *Ps. 143:11*
Bring practical needs and anxieties to the Father

Confession, Forgiveness & Reconciliation
Have mercy on me, O God,
    because of your unfailing love.
Because of your great compassion,
    blot out the stain of my sins. *Ps. 51:1*
Repent to God for wrong done and good left undone

Holiness, Guidance & Protection
Teach me to do your will,
    for you are my God.
May your gracious Spirit lead me forward
    on a firm footing. *Ps. 143:10*
Request the Spirit's wisdom and strength to walk in God's ways

Closing Benediction
    Give thanks to him and praise his name.
For the LORD is good.
    His unfailing love continues forever,
    and his faithfulness continues to each generation. *Ps. 100:4b-5*

Covenant Prayer

Friday - Start of Day
Psalms: 13,22

Moment of Silence
I have calmed and quieted my soul *Ps. 131:2a*

Request for Presence
My God, my God, why have you abandoned me?
  Why are you so far away when I groan for help?
Every day I call to you, my God, but you do not answer.
  Every night I lift my voice, but I find no relief. *Ps. 22:1-2*

Doxology
I will proclaim your name to my brothers and sisters.
  I will praise you among your assembled people. *Ps. 22:22*
Express thankful praise for who God is and what he has done

Gloria Patri

God's Kingdom
The poor will eat and be satisfied.
  All who seek the LORD will praise him.
  Their hearts will rejoice with everlasting joy.
The whole earth will acknowledge the LORD and return to him.
  All the families of the nations will bow down before him.
For royal power belongs to the LORD.
  He rules all the nations. *Ps. 22:26-28*
Pray for God's kingdom to increase locally and globally

Provision
You brought me safely from my mother's womb
  and led me to trust you at my mother's breast.
I was thrust into your arms at my birth.
  You have been my God from the moment I was born. *Ps. 22:9-10*
Bring practical needs and anxieties to the Father

Confession, Forgiveness & Reconciliation
How long must I struggle with anguish in my soul,
  with sorrow in my heart every day?
  How long will my enemy have the upper hand.
Turn and answer me, O LORD my God!
  Restore the sparkle to my eyes, or I will die. *Ps. 13:2-3*
Repent to God for wrong done and good left undone

Holiness, Guidance & Protection
O LORD, do not stay far away!
  You are my strength; come quickly to my aid! *Ps. 22:19*
Request the Spirit's wisdom and strength to walk in God's ways

Closing Benediction
Praise the LORD, all you who fear him! *Ps. 22:23a*

Friday - Lunchtime
Psalms: 54,55

Moment of Silence
I have calmed and quieted my soul *Ps. 131:2a*

Request for Presence
Listen to my prayer, O God.
    Do not ignore my cry for help! *Ps. 55:1*

Doxology
    I will praise your name, O LORD,
    for it is good. *Ps. 54:6b*
Express thankful praise for who God is and what he has done

Gloria Patri

God's Kingdom
    for I see violence and conflict in the city.
Its walls are patrolled day and night against invaders,
    but the real danger is wickedness within the city.
Everything is falling apart *Ps. 55:9b-11a*
Pray for God's kingdom to increase locally and globally

Provision
Give your burdens to the LORD,
    and he will take care of you.
    He will not permit the godly to slip and fall. *Ps. 55:22*
Bring practical needs and anxieties to the Father

Confession, Forgiveness & Reconciliation
Morning, noon, and night
    I cry out in my distress,
    and the LORD hears my voice. *Ps. 55:17*
Repent to God for wrong done and good left undone

Holiness, Guidance & Protection
But God is my helper.
    The Lord keeps me alive! *Ps. 54:4*
Request the Spirit's wisdom and strength to walk in God's ways

Closing Benediction
    I will praise your name, O LORD,
    for it is good.
For you have rescued me from my troubles
    and helped me to triumph over my enemies. *Ps. 54:6b-8*

Friday - Afternoon Break

Moment of Silence
I have calmed and quieted my soul *Ps. 131:2a*

Request for Presence
Now rescue your beloved people.
    Answer and save us by your power. *Ps. 60:5*

Doxology
But you have raised a banner for those who fear you—
    a rallying point in the face of attack. *Ps. 60:4*
Express thankful praise for who God is and what he has done

Gloria Patri

God's Kingdom
You, O God, are my king from ages past,
    bringing salvation to the earth. *Ps. 74:12*
Pray for God's kingdom to increase locally and globally

Provision
Don't let the downtrodden be humiliated again.
    Instead, let the poor and needy praise your name. *Ps. 74:21*
Bring practical needs and anxieties to the Father

Confession, Forgiveness & Reconciliation
O God, why have you rejected us so long?
    Why is your anger so intense against the sheep of your own pasture?
Ps. 74:1
Repent to God for wrong done and good left undone

Holiness, Guidance & Protection
With God's help we will do mighty things,
    for he will trample down our foes. *Ps. 60:12*
Request the Spirit's wisdom and strength to walk in God's ways

Closing Benediction
Have you rejected us, O God?
    Will you no longer march with our armies?
Oh, please help us against our enemies,
    for all human help is useless. *Ps. 60:10-11*

Friday - Dinnertime

Moment of Silence
I have calmed and quieted my soul *Ps. 131:2a*

Request for Presence
Answer my prayers, O LORD,
   for your unfailing love is wonderful.
Take care of me,
   for your mercy is so plentiful. *Ps. 69:16*

Doxology
Then I will praise God's name with singing,
   and I will honor him with thanksgiving.
For this will please the LORD more than sacrificing cattle *Ps. 69:30-31a*
Express thankful praise for who God is and what he has done

Gloria Patri

God's Kingdom
For God will save Jerusalem
   and rebuild the towns of Judah.
His people will live there
   and settle in their own land.
The descendants of those who obey him will inherit the land,
   and those who love him will live there in safety. *Ps. 69:35-36*
Pray for God's kingdom to increase locally and globally

Provision
The humble will see their God at work and be glad.
   Let all who seek God's help be encouraged.
For the LORD hears the cries of the needy;
   he does not despise his imprisoned people. *Ps. 69:32-33*
Bring practical needs and anxieties to the Father

Confession, Forgiveness & Reconciliation
O God, you know how foolish I am;
   my sins cannot be hidden from you.
Don't let those who trust in you be ashamed because of me,
   O Sovereign LORD of Heaven's Armies. *Ps. 69:5-6a*
Repent to God for wrong done and good left undone

Holiness, Guidance & Protection
Let all that I am wait quietly before God,
   for my hope is in him.
He alone is my rock and my salvation,
   my fortress where I will not be shaken.
O my people, trust in him at all times.
   Pour out your heart to him,
   for God is our refuge. *Ps. 62:5-6,8*
Request the Spirit's wisdom and strength to walk in God's ways

Closing Benediction
The humble will see their God at work and be glad.
   Let all who seek God's help be encouraged. *Ps. 69:32*

Saturday - Midnight
Psalms: 47,33,105,119:145-152,107,34,119:161-168

Moment of Silence
I have calmed and quieted my soul Ps. 131:2a

Request for Presence
I rise early, before the sun is up;
   I cry out for help and put my hope in your words. Ps. 119:147

Doxology
Come, everyone! Clap your hands!
   Shout to God with joyful praise!
For the LORD Most High is awesome.
   He is the great King of all the earth. Ps. 47:1-2
Express thankful praise for who God is and what he has done

Gloria Patri

God's Kingdom
The rulers of the world have gathered together
   with the people of the God of Abraham.
For all the kings of the earth belong to God.
   He is highly honored everywhere. Ps. 47:9
Pray for God's kingdom to increase locally and globally

Provision
For he satisfies the thirsty
   and fills the hungry with good things. Ps. 107:9
Bring practical needs and anxieties to the Father

Confession, Forgiveness & Reconciliation
Has the LORD redeemed you? Then speak out!
   Tell others he has redeemed you from your enemies. Ps. 107:2
Repent to God for wrong done and good left undone

Holiness, Guidance & Protection
Does anyone want to live a life
   that is long and prosperous?
Then keep your tongue from speaking evil
   and your lips from telling lies!
Turn away from evil and do good.
   Search for peace, and work to maintain it. Ps. 34:12-14
Request the Spirit's wisdom and strength to walk in God's ways

Closing Benediction
What joy for the nation whose God is the LORD,
   whose people he has chosen as his inheritance. Ps. 33:12

Saturday - Wake Up
Psalms: 8,90,92,149

Moment of Silence
I have calmed and quieted my soul *Ps. 131:2a*

Request for Presence
Satisfy us each morning with your unfailing love,
    so we may sing for joy to the end of our lives. *Ps. 90:14*

Doxology
Praise the LORD!
Sing to the LORD a new song.
    Sing his praises in the assembly of the faithful. *Ps. 149:1*
Express thankful praise for who God is and what he has done

Gloria Patri

God's Kingdom
O LORD, our Lord, your majestic name fills the earth!
    Your glory is higher than the heavens.
You have taught children and infants
    to tell of your strength *Ps. 8:1-2a*
Pray for God's kingdom to increase locally and globally

Provision
But the godly will flourish like palm trees
    and grow strong like the cedars of Lebanon.
For they are transplanted to the LORD's own house.
    They flourish in the courts of our God. *Ps. 92:12-13*
Bring practical needs and anxieties to the Father

Confession, Forgiveness & Reconciliation
You spread out our sins before you—
    our secret sins—and you see them all. *Ps. 90:8*
Repent to God for wrong done and good left undone

Holiness, Guidance & Protection
Teach us to realize the brevity of life,
    so that we may grow in wisdom. *Ps. 90:12*
Request the Spirit's wisdom and strength to walk in God's ways

Closing Benediction
Let us, your servants, see you work again;
    let our children see your glory.
And may the Lord our God show us his approval
    and make our efforts successful.
    Yes, make our efforts successful! *Ps. 90:16-17*

Covenant Prayer

Saturday - Start of Day

Moment of Silence
I have calmed and quieted my soul *Ps. 131:2a*

Request for Presence
   You are so glorious, so majestic!
In your majesty, ride out to victory,
   defending truth, humility, and justice.
   Go forth to perform awe-inspiring deeds!
Your arrows are sharp, piercing your enemies' hearts.
   The nations fall beneath your feet. *Ps. 45:3-5*

Doxology
The heavens proclaim the glory of God.
   The skies display his craftsmanship.
Day after day they continue to speak;
   night after night they make him known. *Ps. 19:1-2*
Express thankful praise for who God is and what he has done

Gloria Patri

God's Kingdom
Your throne, O God, endures forever and ever.
   You rule with a scepter of justice.
You love justice and hate evil. *Ps. 45:6-7a*
Pray for God's kingdom to increase locally and globally

Provision
Your sons will become kings like their father.
   You will make them rulers over many lands. *Ps. 45:16*
Bring practical needs and anxieties to the Father

Confession, Forgiveness & Reconciliation
How can I know all the sins lurking in my heart?
   Cleanse me from these hidden faults.
Keep your servant from deliberate sins!
   Don't let them control me.
Then I will be free of guilt
   and innocent of great sin. *Ps. 19:12-13*
Repent to God for wrong done and good left undone

Holiness, Guidance & Protection
The instructions of the LORD are perfect, reviving the soul.
   The decrees of the LORD are trustworthy, making wise the simple.
The commandments of the LORD are right, bringing joy to the heart.
Ps 19:7-8
Request the Spirit's wisdom and strength to walk in God's ways

Closing Benediction
I will bring honor to your name in every generation.
   Therefore, the nations will praise you forever and ever. *Ps. 45:17*

Saturday - Lunchtime

Psalms: 132,133

Moment of Silence
I have calmed and quieted my soul *Ps. 131:2a*

Request for Presence
Let us go to the sanctuary of the Lord;
    let us worship at the footstool of his throne. *Ps. 132:7*

Doxology
May your priests be clothed in godliness;
    may your loyal servants sing for joy. *Ps. 132:9*
Express thankful praise for who God is and what he has done

Gloria Patri

God's Kingdom
The Lord swore an oath to David
    with a promise he will never take back:
"I will place one of your descendants
    on your throne." *Ps. 132:11*
Pray for God's kingdom to increase locally and globally

Provision
I will bless this city and make it prosperous;
    I will satisfy its poor with food. *Ps. 132:15*
Bring practical needs and anxieties to the Father

Confession, Forgiveness & Reconciliation
How wonderful and pleasant it is
    when brothers live together in harmony! *Ps. 133:1*
Repent to God for wrong done and good left undone

Holiness, Guidance & Protection
If your descendants obey the terms of my covenant
    and the laws that I teach them,
then your royal line
    will continue forever and ever." *Ps. 132:12*
Request the Spirit's wisdom and strength to walk in God's ways

Closing Benediction
The Lord has pronounced his blessing,
    even life everlasting. *Ps. 133:3b*

Saturday - Afternoon Break

Psalms: 85,72,119:169-176

Moment of Silence
I have calmed and quieted my soul *Ps. 131:2a*

Request for Presence
Listen to my prayer;
    rescue me as you promised. *Ps. 119:170*

Doxology
Praise the LORD God, the God of Israel,
    who alone does such wonderful things.
Praise his glorious name forever!
    Let the whole earth be filled with his glory.
Amen and amen! *Ps. 72:18-19*
Express thankful praise for who God is and what he has done

Gloria Patri

God's Kingdom
May there be abundant grain throughout the land,
    flourishing even on the hilltops.
May the fruit trees flourish like the trees of Lebanon,
    and may the people thrive like grass in a field. *Ps. 72:16*
Pray for God's kingdom to increase locally and globally

Provision
Yes, the LORD pours down his blessings.
    Our land will yield its bountiful harvest. *Ps. 85:12*
Bring practical needs and anxieties to the Father

Confession, Forgiveness & Reconciliation
You forgave the guilt of your people—
    yes, you covered all their sins. *Ps. 85:2*
Repent to God for wrong done and good left undone

Holiness, Guidance & Protection
I listen carefully to what God the LORD is saying,
    for he speaks peace to his faithful people.
    But let them not return to their foolish ways. *Ps. 85:8*
Request the Spirit's wisdom and strength to walk in God's ways

Closing Benediction
Unfailing love and truth have met together.
    Righteousness and peace have kissed!
Truth springs up from the earth,
    and righteousness smiles down from heaven.
Yes, the LORD pours down his blessings.
    Our land will yield its bountiful harvest.
Righteousness goes as a herald before him,
    preparing the way for his steps. *Ps. 85:10-13*

Saturday - Dinnertime
Psalms: 27,104,119:105-112

Moment of Silence
I have calmed and quieted my soul *Ps. 131:2a*

Request for Presence
Hear me as I pray, O LORD.
    Be merciful and answer me! *Ps. 27:7*

Doxology
Let all that I am praise the LORD.
O LORD my God, how great you are!
    You are robed with honor and majesty. *Ps. 104:1*
Express thankful praise for who God is and what he has done

Gloria Patri

God's Kingdom
May the glory of the LORD continue forever!
    The LORD takes pleasure in all he has made!
The earth trembles at his glance;
    the mountains smoke at his touch. *Ps. 104:31-32*
Pray for God's kingdom to increase locally and globally

Provision
You cause grass to grow for the livestock
    and plants for people to use.
You allow them to produce food from the earth—
    wine to make them glad,
olive oil to soothe their skin,
    and bread to give them strength. *Ps. 104:14-15*
Bring practical needs and anxieties to the Father

Confession, Forgiveness & Reconciliation
Do not turn your back on me.
    Do not reject your servant in anger.
    You have always been my helper.
Don't leave me now; don't abandon me,
    O God of my salvation! *Ps. 27:9*
Repent to God for wrong done and good left undone

Holiness, Guidance & Protection
The one thing I ask of the LORD—
    the thing I seek most—
is to live in the house of the LORD all the days of my life,
    delighting in the LORD's perfections
    and meditating in his Temple. *Ps. 27:4*
Request the Spirit's wisdom and strength to walk in God's ways

Closing Benediction
Wait patiently for the LORD.
    Be brave and courageous.
    Yes, wait patiently for the LORD. *Ps. 27:11*

Bedtime

Psalms: 4,91,134

I have calmed and quieted my soul *Ps. 131:2a*

Request for Presence
May the Lord Almighty grant me and those I love a peaceful night and a perfect end. Amen.
Our help is in the Name of the Lord; the maker of heaven and earth.

Confession
Almighty God, our heavenly Father: we have sinned against you, through our own fault, in thought, and word, and deed, in what we have done and what we have left undone. For the sake of your Son our Lord Jesus Christ, forgive us all my offenses; and grant that we may serve you in newness of life, to the glory of your Name. Amen.

Psalm 4

Gloria Patri

Psalm 91

Gloria Patri

Psalm 134

The Small Verse
I entrust my spirit into your hand.
    Rescue me, LORD, for you are a faithful God.
Guard me as you would guard your own eyes.
    Hide me in the shadow of your wings. *Ps. 31:5,17:8*

The Lord's Prayer

The Magnificat

Keep watch, dear Lord, with those who work, or watch, or weep tonight, and give Your angels charge over those who sleep. Tend the sick, Lord Christ, give rest to the weary, bless the dying, soothe the suffering, pity the afflicted and shield the joyous, and all for Your love's sake. Amen.

The Prayer of Simeon
Lord, now you are letting your servant depart in peace, according to your word; for my eyes have seen your salvation that you have prepared in the presence of all peoples,
  a light for revelation to the Gentiles,
  and for glory to your people Israel.

Gloria Patri

Appendix I - Common Prayers

The Lord's Prayer

Our Father who is in heaven,
    hallowed be your name
Your kingdom come, Your will be done,
    on earth,
    as it is in heaven.
Give us this day our daily bread
And forgive us our debts,
    as we forgive our debtors
Lead us not into temptation,
    but deliver us from evil.
For yours is the kingdom,
    and the power,
    and the glory forever
Amen

The Shema

Hear, O Israel: The Lord our God, the Lord is one.
You shall love the Lord your God
    with all your heart
    and with all your soul
    and with all your might.
And these words that I command you today shall be on your heart.
You shall teach them diligently to your children,
    and shall talk of them when you sit in your house,
    and when you walk by the way,
    and when you lie down,
    and when you rise.
You shall bind them as a sign on your hand, and they shall be as
frontlets between your eyes. You shall write them on the doorposts of
your house and on your gates.

The Jesus Prayer

Lord Jesus Christ, Son of God,
have mercy on me, a sinner.

Gloria Patri

Glory be to God the Father, God the Son, and God the Holy Spirit. As it
was in the beginning, so it is now and so it shall ever be, world without
end. Alleluia. Amen.

Sanctus

Holy, holy, holy Lord, God of power and might,
heaven and earth are full of your glory.
Hosanna in the highest.
Blessed is he who comes in the name of the Lord.
Hosanna in the highest.

The Magnificat

Oh, how my soul praises the Lord.
How my spirit rejoices in God my Savior!
For he took notice of his lowly servant girl,
and from now on all generations will call me blessed.
For the Mighty One is holy,
and he has done great things for me.
He shows mercy from generation to generation
to all who fear him.
His mighty arm has done tremendous things!
He has scattered the proud and haughty ones.
He has brought down princes from their thrones
and exalted the humble.
He has filled the hungry with good things
and sent the rich away with empty hands.
He has helped his servant Israel
and remembered to be merciful.
For he made this promise to our ancestors,
to Abraham and his children forever.

The Prayer of St. Francis

Lord, make me an instrument of your peace!
That where there is hatred, I may bring love.
That where there is wrong, I may bring the spirit of forgiveness.
That where there is discord, I may bring harmony.
That where there is error, I may bring truth.
That where there is doubt, I may bring faith.
That where there is despair, I may bring hope.
That where there are shadows, I may bring light.
That where there is sadness, I may bring joy.
Lord, grant that I may seek rather to comfort, than to be comforted.
To understand, than to be understood.
To love, than to be loved.
For it is by self-forgetting that one finds.
It is by forgiving that one is forgiven.
It is by dying that one awakens to Eternal Life.

The Covenant Prayer - John Wesley

I am no longer my own, but Yours:
Put me to what You will, rank me with whom You will;
Put me to doing, put me to suffering;
Let me be employed by You or laid aside for You;
Exalted for You or brought low by You;
Let me be full, let me empty;
Let me have all things, let me have nothing.
I freely and heartily yield all things to Your pleasure and disposal.
And now, O glorious and blessed God,
Father, Son and Holy Spirit,
You are mine, and I am Yours.
So be it. Amen.

Heidelberg Catechism Q&A 1

What is your only comfort in life and in death?
That I belong, both body and soul and in life and in death, not to myself, but to my faithful savior Jesus Christ, who has totally paid for all my sins with his precious blood and completely liberated me from the power of the devil, and who takes care of me so well that not a hair can fall from my head without the will of my Father in heaven. In fact, everything must work together for my salvation. Besides this, by his Holy Spirit he also assures me of eternal life and makes me wholeheartedly willing and ready to live for him from now on.

Prayer to the Holy Spirit - St. Augustine

Breathe in me O Holy Spirit,
    that my thoughts may all be holy.
Act in me O Holy Spirit,
    that my work, too, may be holy.
Draw my heart O Holy Spirit,
    that I love but what is holy.
Strengthen me O Holy Spirit,
    to defend all that is holy.
Guard me, then, O Holy Spirit,
    that I always may be holy. Amen.

St. Patrick's Breastplate

Christ with me,
Christ before me,
Christ behind me,
Christ in me,
Christ beneath me,
Christ above me,
Christ on my right,
Christ on my left,
Christ when I lie down,
Christ when I sit down,
Christ when I arise,
Christ in the heart of every man who thinks of me,
Christ in the mouth of everyone who speaks of me,
Christ in every eye that sees me,
Christ in every ear that hears me.

Prayer for the Sick - St. Augustine

Watch, dear Lord, with those who wake, or watch,
or weep tonight, and let your angels protect those who sleep.
Tend the sick.
Refresh the weary.
Sustain the dying.
Calm the suffering.
Pity the distressed.
We ask this for the sake of your love.
Amen.

Appendix II - Spiritual Exercises

The following is a small sampling of spiritual practices that have been used throughout history. They can be powerful guides in strengthening your own study and prayer habits and have been included in brief forms for convenience.

Lectio Divina

Lectio Divina, or Sacred Reading, is a simple practice blending prayer and scripture in order to bring God's word into your *heart*. You take a small section of scripture that you generally understand, typically no more than two or three verses, and bring it through the following four phases over around 15-30 minutes on average:

Reading (Lectio)

Read the text slowly. The ancient practice was to read the text through four times, each time emphasizing a different aspect.

Meditation (Meditatio)

Ruminating and reflecting on the text. What does it say about God? People? Myself? What is it challenging in me? Where am I afraid? What excites me?

Prayer (Oratio)

Talk to God about your reflections. Is there something to thank God for? Sin to confess? A promise to trust? A specific step of obedience to take?

Contemplation (Contemplatio)

Finish with a few minutes of silence. This is a time of simply resting "Coram Deo" (in the presence of God).

Further reading

- Eat This Book: A Conversation in the Art of Spiritual Reading - *Eugene Peterson*
- Opening to God: Lectio Divina and Life as Prayer - *David G. Benner*
- Lectio Divina: The Medieval Experience of Reading (Cistercian Studies) - *Duncan Robertson*
- Lectio Divina: How to Pray Sacred Scripture - *Dan Korn*

The Examen

The Examen is a simple prayer of reflection, typically done at the end of the day. In our busy world, it can be a valuable tool to intentionally slow down and see where we may have missed the recent subtle movements of the Spirit in our lives. The Examen is broken into five movements:

Invitation

Take a few deep breaths and quiet your mind. Ask the Spirit to be present, and for the ability to discern his voice and will.

Gratitude

Praise God through thankfulness for 1 or 2 things. This can be anything - something specific that occurred in the day, an unexpected blessing, answer to prayer, a relationship. Try to think of small things as well as the big ones. Thanking God for a stranger's smile or a good cup of coffee is perfectly acceptable.

Review

This is the heart of the prayer. Beginning when you first wake up, slowly and prayerfully scan through your day looking for times you acted out of fear or love, anxiety or faith. Make note of patterns that emerge regularly.

Looking forward

Identify 1 or 2 thought or behavior patterns that stuck out to you to discuss with God. Repent where necessary and request his help to grow in those areas going forward.

Close

Thank God for the day and commit the remainder of the night to him. Close with the Lord's Prayer.

Further reading

- The Jesuit Guide to (Almost) Everything: A Spirituality for Real Life - *Father James Martin SJ*
- Reimagining the Ignatian Examen: Fresh Ways to Pray from Your Day - *Father Mark E. Thibodeaux SJ*
- The Spiritual Exercises of Saint Ignatius: Saint Ignatius' Profound Precepts of Mystical Theology - *St. Ignatius of Loyola*

Reading Scripture for Change

In Matthew 7, Jesus tells the parable of the two people, a wise man and a foolish man. The wise man builds his house on a sturdy foundation while the fool builds on shifting sand. At the end of the parable, Jesus explains that both the wise man and the fool have **heard** his words, but only the wise man **obeyed** his word. Reading scripture must not be an intellectual exercise of the mind, but a practical one that changes our thoughts, actions and attitudes. Below is a simple process for ensuring our time in God's word leads to real change.

Read
Read the passage a couple of times. It can be helpful to use two or more translations. Spend a minute looking into any unfamiliar words or concepts but be careful not to get pulled into a rabbit trail!

Retell
Write down or explain in a group what you think the passage means *in your own words*. Being able to retell the main ideas of the passage in your own words is crucial in both learning and application.

Looking Up
What is God saying? What does it mean? Why is it included in Scripture? What does it say about God, Jesus or the Holy Spirit? The Story of the Kingdom? Humans? The World?

Looking Inside
What is God saying *to me*?
What is sticking out to me? Why?
Where do I see evidence of grace in my life in this area? Where in my life do I see opportunities for growth?

Looking Ahead
What am I going to do about it?
What practical step forward am I committing to taking this week?
Is there someone I should share this with?

Share your learnings with a trusted friend or community and invite their prayers and support. Accountability is a key component of growing in maturity.

Appendix III - Prayer Notes

The following blank pages are designed to keep track of ongoing prayer requests. To aid in recalling specific requests during particular extemporaneous sections of the office, the various headings are provided for convenience.

Doxology
Our Father, who is in Heaven, hallowed be your name

What have you seen God do lately that you wish to thank him for?

_____

_____

_____

_____

_____

_____

_____

_____

_____

_____

_____

_____

_____

_____

_____

_____

_____

_____

_____

_____

_____

_____

God's Kingdom

Your Kingdom come, your will be done on Earth as it is in Heaven

Who do you long to see in God's family? Who is actively laboring in the Kingdom? What opportunities exist for healing, service, and tangible love?

_____

_____

_____

_____

_____

_____

_____

_____

_____

_____

_____

_____

_____

_____

_____

_____

_____

_____

_____

_____

_____

_____

Provision
Give us this day, our daily bread

What day-to-day needs and anxieties are keeping you up?

_____

_____

_____

_____

_____

_____

_____

_____

_____

_____

_____

_____

_____

_____

_____

_____

_____

_____

_____

_____

_____

_____

Forgiveness & Reconciliation

Forgive us our sins as we forgive those who have sinned against us

What do you need forgiveness for? Who do you need to forgive? What broken relationships do you long to see restored?

_____

_____

_____

_____

_____

_____

_____

_____

_____

_____

_____

_____

_____

_____

_____

_____

_____

_____

_____

_____

_____

_____

Holiness, Guidance & Protection
And lead us not into temptation, but deliver us from the Evil one

Where are you tempted, ensnared, or fearful?

CPSIA information can be obtained
at www.ICGtesting.com
Printed in the USA
LVHW082128020621
689027LV00029B/448